Soft Skills

Geo Report
2023

Chapter 1: Unlocking the Power of Soft Skills

In a world in constant evolution, where achievements go beyond technical skills, there is a set of skills that stands out as the true differential - the Soft Skills. They are the hidden cogs that drive success in all areas of life, from professionalism to interpersonal relationships. In this first chapter, embark with us on a journey of discovery to understand what these subtle but powerful skills are and why they are essential in today's landscape.

We will enter the world of Soft Skills, revealing their roots and deep meaning. We'll go beneath the surface, exploring the transcendent importance they have in our careers, social interactions and self-improvement. You'll understand the vital distinction between Soft Skills and Hard Skills, and how this balance is key to a successful career.

As we dive into this introductory chapter, we set the stage for an enriching journey. Get ready to discover the hidden facets that shape our ability to lead, collaborate, innovate and thrive in a world where Soft Skills have become the fundamental pillars of excellence.

1. What are Soft Skills?

Now, let's explore the core of Soft Skills. But what exactly are these skills, as subtle as they are essential? Think of them as the symphony of emotional intelligence, the dance of effective communication, and the foundation of successful interpersonal relationships. They are the non-technical skills that transcend curricula and certificates, directly influencing our ability to navigate the complex world we live in.

These refined skills go beyond technical and scientific prowess. They understand our ability to communicate clearly and empathetically, to understand and manage our own emotions as well as the emotions of those around us. They are the root of charismatic leadership, fruitful collaboration and creative thinking that revolutionizes industries.

Soft Skills are the adornment that enhances our professional etiquette, our ability to resolve conflicts and adapt to changes in the global scenario. They enable us to interact harmoniously in diverse environments, to inspire and motivate colleagues, to make wise decisions and to learn from each experience.

Understanding what Soft Skills are is the first step towards unlocking your maximum potential. They are not just a collection of vague traits, but the skills that make us complete as professionals and human beings. In this chapter, we'll delve deeper into that essence, unraveling the subtleties and nuances that make up the splendor of Soft Skills, and thus prepare ourselves to explore how to develop and apply them in our everyday lives.

2. The importance of Soft Skills in today's world

As the wheels of the modern world turn with unprecedented intensity, an undeniable truth emerges: Soft Skills have become the pillars that underpin success in our complex and interconnected society. They are the crucial element that transforms a competent professional into an inspiring leader, a team into an unstoppable creative force and a work environment into a stronghold of harmony and innovation.

In the global scenario, where borders are increasingly tenuous and communication crosses continents in a matter of seconds, technical skills, although fundamental, are no longer enough. Soft Skills, with their ability to build bridges across cultures, manage conflicts with grace, and express ideas in an engaging way, emerge as the currency of universal value.

Leading companies in the market have recognized the invaluable importance of Soft Skills, and the value that these skills confer on their employees. From leadership to the bottom line, from creativity to problem solving, Soft Skills have infiltrated every corner of successful organizations, boosting effectiveness, cohesion and adaptability.

Beyond corporate doors, these transcendent skills also shape our relationships, our ability to lead diverse teams, make sound decisions in an ever-evolving world, and maintain resilience in the face of unforeseen challenges.

Deep into the importance of Soft Skills in the contemporary world. We will understand how they became the difference between success and stagnation, how they directly impact our ability to progress professionally and how, with mastery, we can cultivate and apply them in our lives. By mastering these skills, we open doors to a future filled with achievements and opportunities that transcend the boundaries of what is merely technical.

3. Difference between Soft Skills and Hard Skills

To understand the true landscape of skills that drive success, it is essential to discern the difference between Soft Skills and Hard Skills. While Hard Skills are like solid foundations, representing our technical knowledge, Soft Skills are the veneer that enriches these foundations, shaping our interpersonal effectiveness and adaptability.

Hard Skills are tangible and measurable, referring to the set of specific skills that we can acquire through training, education and direct experience. These are the technical skills we see listed on resumes, certificates and diplomas, such as proficiency in programming, aptitude for financial analysis or the ability to operate complex machinery.

Soft Skills are more subtle, but no less vital. They encompass our ability to communicate effectively, to work as a team, to resolve conflicts diplomatically and to adapt to changing scenarios. It's skills like emotional intelligence, empathy, critical thinking and leadership that influence our social interactions, our flexibility and our success in the workplace.

While Hard Skills allow us to perform specific tasks, Soft Skills determine how well we perform those tasks and how well we connect with others. Balancing these two skill categories is critical to a successful career and life.

This distinction in depth. Let's understand how Hard Skills open doors and Soft Skills ensure we walk through those doors with confidence. By understanding the synergy between these two types of skills, we will be one step closer to mastering the full game, building not just a solid foundation, but a complete building of competencies that will lead us to lasting success.

4. How Soft Skills impact your career and personal life

The transforming power of Soft Skills transcends the boundaries of the professional environment, reaching the dimensions of our personal lives. They are not just honed skills for a resume, but the threads that weave the tapestry of a solid career and a life filled with meaningful relationships.

Imagine, for a moment, the professional scene. With honed Soft Skills, you become a leadership force, able to inspire and motivate your team, make wise decisions at crucial moments, and maintain resilience in the face of challenges. Their ability to communicate clearly and empathetically creates connections that transcend hierarchies, facilitating collaboration and building a healthy organizational culture.

Soft Skills also manifest as your trump card in negotiation and conflict resolution situations. Your emotional intelligence allows you to navigate the turbulent waters of adversity with grace, while your ability to empathize creates fertile ground for authentic, collaborative relationships.

Now broaden the focus to the personal sphere. Here, Soft Skills shine as your most valuable allies. Empathy strengthens family ties and friendships, effective communication maintains harmony in relationships, and your adaptability allows you to flourish in the face of life's inevitable changes.

The balance between career and personal life, so essential these days, is also influenced by Soft Skills. Your ability to manage time, set healthy boundaries, and handle stress become the cornerstones of a balanced and fulfilled life.

In the Soft Skills web of influence, exploring how they shape professional trajectories and personal well-being. You'll understand how each skill not only plays an individual role, but how together they create a synergistic impact that transcends the barriers between career and personal life. By understanding this impact, you will be armed with the knowledge you need to cultivate and apply these skills in both domains, reaping the rewards of a truly fulfilling life.

5. Main Soft Skills valued by companies

At the center of attention of visionary companies are Soft Skills, the pearls that stand out in an ocean of talented candidates. These subtle but decisive competencies have become the selection criteria for those organizations that seek not only skilled professionals, but also individuals capable of driving innovation, building strong relationships and adapting with agility.

Leadership is one of the Soft Skills that shines brightly in the eyes of companies. The ability to inspire, motivate and guide a team towards shared goals is invaluable. Skilled leaders not only lead with mastery, but also nurture an environment of trust and mutual respect, maximizing the potential of everyone around them.

Effective communication is another highly valued skill. The ability to convey ideas clearly, listen carefully and adapt to the audience is an asset that allows for fluid collaboration, successful negotiation and building a culture of open communication.

Critical thinking and problem solving are Soft Skills that provide the company with the ability to face complex challenges. Individuals who can analyze situations, make data-driven decisions and propose innovative solutions are true catalysts for growth and evolution.

Empathy, often underestimated, is a quality that does not go unnoticed by progressive companies. The ability to understand others' perspectives and needs, collaborate effectively, and build strong relationships strengthens team cohesion and creates a more inclusive work environment.

Last but not least, adaptability is a Soft Skill that has become essential in an ever-changing world. Professionals who can embrace new challenges, learn quickly and adapt to unforeseen scenarios are the foundation of organizational resilience.

These Soft Skills in detail, understanding how they shape the vision of companies and become the differentiating criterion between a promising candidate and a potential leader. By mastering these valued skills, you will be one step ahead on the journey to success in the corporate world and be able to stand out in a highly competitive landscape.

Chapter 2: Effective Communication

Communication, the essence of human connection, is the foundation on which we build strong relationships, convey brilliant ideas, and influence the course of history. Mastering the art of effective communication is like holding a magic wand that opens doors, breaks down barriers and creates lasting bonds.

In this chapter, we'll dive into the waters of communication, exploring every facet of this essential skill. From verbal to non-verbal communication, we will understand how each word, each gesture and even silence can convey deep meanings and impact the perception of others.

Active listening, a rare pearl in a sea of noise, is one of the most valuable gems of effective communication. Through it, we not only listen, but really understand what is being said, allowing us to respond in a more empathetic and constructive way. Empathy, a vital component of communication, allows us to immerse ourselves in others' experiences, building bridges between hearts and minds.

But communication is not just limited to words. Written communication, in today's digital world, is a fundamental skill. The ability to express yourself clearly, concisely and persuasively in emails, reports and documents is an asset that drives progress in any sphere.

Furthermore, we cannot ignore interpersonal communication, the complex dance of facial expressions, body language and non-verbal language that shapes our daily interactions. Mastering this dance is essential for creating lasting relationships, transmitting trust and creating a harmonious work environment.

Effective communication is the bridge that takes us from conflict resolution to fruitful negotiation. It allows us to articulate our ideas, influence decisions and drive change in a persuasive way. In this chapter, we'll explore the roots of effective communication, delving into the skills that make it up and understanding how to cultivate them in our everyday lives. As we master this art, we will be prepared to positively influence our environment, lead with mastery and create an authentic connection with others.

1. Verbal communication skills

The ability to express yourself verbally with dexterity is one of the master keys to open the doors of success, whether in the professional world or in personal relationships. Verbal communication is the symphony of words, the choreography of language, the way in which we convey our thoughts, ideas and emotions in a clear, engaging and persuasive way.

Clarity is the foundation on which we build effective communication. The ability to express our ideas coherently, concisely and understandably is like dropping an anchor in a sea of confusion, allowing our messages to hit home.

Persuasion, a powerful tool, is another crucial facet of verbal communication. The ability to argue convincingly, articulate our reasons solidly, and adapt our approach to the audience is like a spell that envelops and influences others.

Tone of voice, rhythm and intonation are elements that bring our words to life. They convey emotions, reflect confidence and determine the underlying message. Learning to modulate these elements is like tuning an instrument, allowing us to create harmony in our interactions.

Attentive listening, often overlooked, is one of the golden keys to effective communication. It is through listening that we not only understand, but also show respect and empathy. By listening with genuine interest, we make room for deeper connections and build solid relationships.

The constant practice and improvement of these skills lead us to a level of eloquence and impact. In this chapter, we'll delve into the waters of verbal communication, understanding how each component intertwines to create a powerful message. As we master these skills, we will be prepared to unlock the secrets of communication that not only conveys information, but also inspires, persuades and positively influences the world around us.

2. Non-verbal communication skills

On the stage of human interactions, there is a subtle and powerful language that transcends words. It is the non-verbal communication skills that, like a skilled painter, add depth and nuance to our communications, making them richer, more expressive and authentic.

We'll start with the fascinating universe of body language, where gestures, posture and facial expressions communicate feelings and intentions in a vivid and immediate way. Learning to read and interpret these signals allows us to understand the emotions and attitudes behind words, revealing deeper layers of meaning.

Eye contact, often called "the window to the soul," is one of the gems of nonverbal skills. The gaze can convey empathy, confidence, sincerity, or disinterest. The ability to respectfully and sincerely maintain eye contact is a vital component of communication that builds strong and lasting connections.

Paralanguage, the set of elements that accompany speech, such as tone of voice, rhythm, pauses and emphasis, is a rich source of non-verbal information. It can convey feelings, indicate confidence levels or reveal emotional states. Learning to adjust the paralanguage according to the context and the audience is a powerful tool to convey our messages effectively.

Personal spaces, touches, and other elements of physical context are also part of the realm of nonverbal communication. They affect our perception and interactions, shaping the dynamics of relationships. Understanding how these elements influence communication allows us to create environments conducive to positive interactions.

Mastering non-verbal communication skills is like mastering a secret language. It's the ability to read between the lines, tune in to emotional nuances, and subtly influence the environment. In this chapter, we will unravel these skills, understanding how they complement verbal communication, enriching our relationships and allowing us to communicate in a more complete, impactful and authentic way.

3. Active listening and empathy

In a world filled with voices clamoring for attention, the true art of active listening stands out like a rare gem, capable of transforming our interactions from superficial to meaningful. Accompanied by empathy, this skill creates a symphony of understanding and connection, enriching our relationships and making us truly present in the moment.

Active listening, more than a mere action, is an attitude. It is the conscious act of giving our full attention to the speaker, letting go of distractions and judgments, and tuning in to the words and emotions that are being shared. It is through this listening that we genuinely understand the message being conveyed, not just the words but the underlying feelings as well.

But active listening transcends mere understanding. She is an invitation to the other to express herself fully, to feel heard and valued. It is a manifestation of respect and genuine interest, an act that builds bridges between people, nurturing trust and strengthening bonds.

Empathy is the natural corollary of active listening. It is the ability to put yourself in the other's shoes, to understand their perspectives, emotions and needs. Empathy allows us to create deep connections, demonstrating that we really care about the experiences and feelings of others.

But empathy is not limited to understanding; it extends to action. It is the basis on which we build solidary and respectful relationships. Through it, we can offer support, compassion and encouragement, building an environment where people feel understood and supported.

The harmony of active listening and the poetry of empathy. We'll learn how to cultivate these skills, how to apply them in our daily interactions, and how they can elevate our communication to a level of depth and meaning. By mastering this art, we will be prepared to build more authentic relationships, resolve conflicts with grace and create an environment where people feel valued and understood.

4. Written and digital communication

In today's world, where words flow across screens and keyboards, mastering the art of written communication is like having a magic pen capable of tracing impactful messages and reaching vast audiences. In this chapter, we'll delve into the essence of written communication and explore the nuances of the digital landscape, where every written word has the power to create connections, influence and convey our message beyond physical barriers.

Written communication requires a careful look at the words we choose. Each sentence is a piece of a puzzle, building a cohesive and engaging narrative. Clarity, conciseness, and proper grammar are the tools of the skilled writer, allowing messages to be understood effortlessly.

Adapting to the digital landscape is crucial in a world where communication flows through emails, text messages, social networks and collaborative platforms. The ability to convey our ideas effectively in this environment requires not only technical skills, but also a deep understanding of how tone, context, and formatting impact the interpretation of messages.

Engaging writing, capable of capturing attention and inspiring action, is a precious art. It is through it that we can influence and persuade, sharing ideas and values in a powerful way. The ability to tell stories, to present convincing arguments and to convey our message in a captivating way is a valuable tool in any sphere.

But written communication goes beyond persuasion. It is also the foundation on which we build solid professional and personal relationships. The ability to express empathy, offer constructive feedback and collaborate effectively through writing is an asset that allows us to create authentic connections, even from a distance.

The nuances of written communication, understanding how its unique characteristics shape our interactions and impact our reach. We'll learn how to adapt our writing to the digital landscape, how to convey our message in a clear and engaging way, and how to use this skill to create lasting relationships and positively influence the world around us. By mastering the dance of words, we will be equipped to communicate effectively, regardless of medium, and to leave our mark on the digital pages of history.

5. Dealing with conflicts and negotiations

In the complex web of human interactions, conflict arises as an inevitable challenge. However, the way we approach these conflicts and the ability to negotiate masterfully can turn chaos into opportunities for growth, collaboration and constructive resolution.

Dealing with conflict requires the ability to stay calm in the midst of the storm, understand conflicting perspectives, and find solutions that satisfy all parties involved. Empathetic communication is a valuable tool in this scenario, allowing us to listen to concerns and feelings on all sides, building a foundation for mutual understanding.

Conflict resolution is a delicate dance, where empathy and assertiveness intertwine. It is the balance between expressing our own interests and understanding the interests of others. It is the search for creative solutions that meet everyone's needs, creating an atmosphere of collaboration and respect.

Negotiations, on the other hand, are a high form of art. They require thorough preparation, understanding the goals and interests of the parties involved, and the ability to communicate persuasively. Effective negotiation is like a chessboard, where every move is calculated to reach the desired goal.

Empathy is the essence of successful negotiation, allowing us to build trusting relationships, understand the other side's needs and concerns, and find solutions that benefit both. The ability to give in without compromising our own goals, to seek mutual gains and to maintain a climate of respect are the pillars of an ethical and productive negotiation.

In the art of diplomacy, understanding how to handle conflicts constructively and negotiate masterfully. We will learn to create an environment conducive to conflict resolution, to apply effective negotiation techniques and to cultivate empathy as a valuable tool to build bridges between the parties. By mastering these skills, we will be prepared to face challenges, seize opportunities and create an environment of collaboration, growth and mutual respect.

Chapter 3: Emotional Intelligence

In the vast landscape of human abilities, emotional intelligence emerges as a guiding star, illuminating our journey to self-knowledge, interpersonal success and emotional well-being. It is the ability to understand, manage and use emotions as a driving force, allowing us to navigate the turbulent waters of life with grace and determination.

Emotional intelligence begins with self-awareness, the ability to look within ourselves and understand our own emotions, motivations and reactions. It is the awakening of awareness of our emotional states, allowing us to identify when we are happy, sad, anxious or excited.

In addition to self-knowledge, emotional intelligence encompasses self-management, the ability to control our emotions in a healthy and constructive way. This entails dealing with stress effectively, staying calm in challenging situations, and channeling our emotions appropriately, whether it's finding solutions or expressing understanding.

Empathy, an essential facet of emotional intelligence, is the ability to tune in to the emotions of others, understand their perspectives, and show genuine interest. Empathy allows us to build solid relationships, demonstrating understanding and solidarity.

The ability to manage relationships is another dimension of emotional intelligence. It is the ability to build healthy relationships, resolve conflicts constructively, and positively influence others. This requires effective communication, the ability to listen empathetically, and the ability to collaborate as a team.

The symphony of emotions that make up emotional intelligence. We will understand how to develop self-awareness, how to manage our emotions in a healthy way, how to cultivate empathy and how to build solid relationships. By mastering this skill, we will be equipped to face emotional challenges with confidence, create authentic connections with others, and pave the way to personal growth and interpersonal success.

1. Recognizing and managing emotions

Emotions, like currents that guide us through life, are an essential component of our humanity. The ability to recognize and manage these currents is like mastering a rudder, allowing us to deftly navigate the shifting seas of emotional experience.

Recognizing emotions begins by looking closely inside ourselves. It is the ability to identify and name what we are feeling, understanding the breadth of our emotional spectrum. It's noticing when anxiety whispers, when joy shines, when sadness envelops or when anger sparks.

Going deeper into the complexity of our emotions allows us to unravel the roots that sustain them, the underlying causes that often remain veiled. This allows us to understand the reason for our reactions, creating space for more conscious management.

Managing emotions is a subtle art, involving the ability to respond rather than react impulsively. It's recognizing that we are the captains of our emotions, choosing how to respond to each situation. This requires emotional resilience, the ability to deal with adversity, and the flexibility to adapt to change.

Emotion regulation, a pillar of emotional management, allows us to find the balance between expressing our emotions in a healthy way and remaining calm when necessary. This involves techniques such as practicing mindfulness, seeking out relaxing activities, and developing a set of strategies for coping with stress.

Authenticity is an essential part of this process. Recognizing and managing emotions does not mean repressing them, but allowing them to flow naturally, expressing them constructively. This implies being honest with yourself and others, creating a foundation for more genuine and healthy relationships.

The art of recognizing and managing emotions, understanding how each aspect fits into the puzzle of our emotional experience. We will learn to cultivate self-awareness, to respond consciously to our emotions and to create an internal environment where emotional currents flow with harmony and purpose. By mastering this skill, we will be prepared to face the emotional tides of life with serenity, resilience and authenticity.

2. Self-awareness and emotional self-management

At the center of our existence, there is a vast and fascinating territory: our own being. The journey to explore this territory, understanding our emotions, motivations and reactions, is a sacred quest that leads us to a place of authenticity, balance and resilience. It is the domain of self-knowledge, combined with emotional self-management, that enables us to navigate with dexterity through the tumultuous waters of life.

Self-knowledge is the light that illuminates the deepest corners of our soul. It's the ability to look inside ourselves, question our beliefs, understand our values and recognize the origins of our emotions. It is a journey of self-exploration that allows us to unravel the mysteries that shape our thoughts and behavior.

By knowing ourselves, we gain the power to recognize our emotions clearly and without judgment. We learn to identify when we are sad, when we are happy, when we are anxious, when we are excited and much more. This creates a space of authenticity, allowing us to be honest about our emotional states and build more genuine relationships.

Emotional self-management, a natural extension of self-awareness, is the ability to consciously respond to our emotions. It's like holding the reins of our inner horse, directing our reactions in healthy and constructive ways. This does not mean repressing emotions, but recognizing them, understanding them, and choosing how to respond to them.

Self-management allows us to find a balance between expressing our emotions in a healthy way and remaining calm when necessary. This involves looking for strategies to deal with stress, practicing self-compassion, and developing an arsenal of techniques to promote emotional well-being.

The inner journey, understanding how self-knowledge is the key to unlocking the secrets of our emotional nature and how self-management allows us to walk a path of resilience, balance and authenticity. By mastering these skills, we will be prepared to face life's complexities with renewed clarity, a conscious response to emotions, and the ability to navigate the waters of our existence with grace.

3. Empathy and social skills

On the stage of human relations, empathy emerges as a beacon of understanding, an invisible link that connects us to the experiences and emotions of others. It is the ability to feel and understand what others are experiencing, to tune in to their perspectives, and to show a genuine interest in the well-being of others. Allied to this empathy, social skills are like the wings that allow us to fly in the currents of human interactions, building solid and effective relationships.

Empathy starts with the simple act of listening carefully. It is the respectful silence we offer, allowing the voices of others to be heard. By listening with genuine interest, we not only capture the words, but also the underlying emotions, creating an environment of trust and understanding.

But empathy goes beyond listening. It involves the ability to put yourself in others' shoes, to understand their perspectives and reactions. It is the process of validating others' emotions, of showing that we recognize and understand what they are feeling. This strengthens bonds, creates a supportive atmosphere, and allows people to feel understood and valued.

Social skills, in turn, are the fundamental building blocks of healthy and effective relationships. They include effective communication, the ability to express our ideas clearly and to listen carefully to the ideas of others. They also cover assertiveness, which allows us to express our thoughts and feelings respectfully, and conflict resolution, which helps us face interpersonal challenges with grace and poise.

Empathy and social skills complement each other, creating an environment of mutual respect, collaboration and understanding. Empathy is the foundation, while soft skills are the tools we use to build bridges between people. In this chapter, we'll explore the art of the heart, understanding how to cultivate empathy, improve social skills, and create a space of authentic and harmonious relationships. By mastering these skills, we will be prepared to face interpersonal challenges with compassion, confidence and skill, strengthening the connections that enrich our lives.

4. Dealing with stress and pressure

In the frantic pace of modern life, where demands accumulate and responsibilities multiply, stress and pressure become frequent companions on our journey. However, how we approach these challenges can determine our ability to remain calm, preserve mental health and achieve a balance that allows us to thrive, even in the most turbulent times.

Dealing with stress starts with being aware of our own reactions. It is the recognition of when we feel overwhelmed, anxious or drained. Self-observation is the key to noticing the first signs of stress, allowing us to take preventive measures before it reaches disproportionate proportions.

Self-compassion is a valuable resource in this process. It is the ability to treat ourselves with kindness and understanding, recognizing that we all, at some point, face challenges and times of pressure. Self-compassion allows us to alleviate self-criticism and judgment, creating a space for self-care and resilience.

Time management is a key tool for dealing with pressure. It is the ability to prioritize, set boundaries and be effective in organizing tasks. Time management allows us to find a balance between professional and personal responsibilities, avoiding the feeling of overload and exhaustion.

In addition, the practice of mindfulness is a powerful ally in reducing stress. It is the ability to be present in the moment, to observe thoughts and emotions without judgment. Mindfulness helps us find an oasis of serenity amidst the hustle and bustle, allowing us to face challenges with more mental clarity.

Strategies for dealing with stress and pressure, understanding how self-awareness, self-compassion, time management and mindfulness are the tools that enable us to face the whirlwinds of life with balance and resilience. By mastering these techniques, we will be able to navigate the tumultuous waters with grace, preserving our mental health and finding a peaceful space in the midst of chaos.

5. Building healthy interpersonal relationships

Amid the complex fabric of life, interpersonal relationships are the threads that unite individuals, forming networks of connections that enrich our existence. The ability to build healthy relationships is a valuable art, a dance that requires empathy, effective communication and a deep respect for the individuality of each human being. In this chapter, we'll delve into the depths of this art, unlocking the secrets to forging relationships that nourish, strengthen, and light our path.

Empathy, like a golden thread that weaves relationships together, is the ability to tune in to the emotions and perspectives of others. It is the art of listening attentively, of putting yourself in the other's shoes, of recognizing and validating the experiences of others. Empathy is the essence of understanding, creating a space where people feel valued and understood.

Communication is the foundation on which we build solid relationships. Effective communication involves the ability to express our thoughts and feelings clearly and respectfully while being able to listen carefully to what others have to say. It is the pursuit of clarity, the use of non-violent language and a willingness to resolve misunderstandings constructively.

Respect for the individuality of each person is a fundamental pillar. It is the acceptance that we are all unique, with our own perspectives, beliefs and values. Respect allows us to build bridges, find common ground and celebrate the diversity that enriches our lives.

Conflict resolution, an inevitable part of the human relations journey, is an essential skill. It is the ability to face disagreements with maturity, seeking solutions that satisfy all parties involved. Conflict resolution requires empathy, effective communication and the ability to seek mutual understanding.

The keys to building healthy interpersonal relationships, understanding how empathy, effective communication, respect for individuality and conflict resolution are the elements that shape the quality of our connections. We will learn to cultivate these skills, nurture authentic relationships, and create an environment where relationships flourish, bringing joy, support, and mutual growth. By mastering this art, we will be prepared to build lasting and meaningful bonds that enrich our journey.

Chapter 4: Leadership and Management

In the dynamic landscape of business and life, leadership emerges like a beacon, illuminating the path to excellence and inspiring the pursuit of progress. In addition to commanding, leadership is the ability to influence, guide and create an environment where people feel motivated and empowered to achieve their goals. In this same context, management is a skillful art, the mastery of coordinating resources, time and efforts effectively. Together, leadership and management are like the pillars that underpin an organization's structure, shaping culture, driving performance and building a vibrant future.

Leadership transcends formal authority. It's the ability to inspire and influence, to convey a compelling vision that resonates with people's hearts and minds. It is building a culture of trust, where integrity and example are the foundations. An authentic leader is one who listens, guides and supports, valuing the potential of each individual.

Empathy is a powerful ally in leadership, allowing the leader to understand the needs and concerns of team members. It is the ability to put yourself in others' shoes, to recognize their perspectives, and to show a genuine interest in their well-being. Empathy creates an environment where people feel valued and understood, increasing cohesion and collaboration.

But leadership isn't just about inspiring; it also involves practical management skills. It is the balance between strategic vision and efficient execution. Effective management requires the ability to plan, organize and delegate responsibilities clearly and efficiently. It is the intelligent use of available resources to achieve goals and objectives.

Team management, a crucial aspect of management, requires sensitivity and respect for individuals. It's the ability to motivate, give constructive feedback, and resolve conflicts with grace. A well-managed team is like a cohesive organism, with each member contributing their unique skills toward a common goal.

The universe of leadership and management, understanding how authentic leadership inspires, empathy connects, and effective management enables goal achievement. We will learn to cultivate these skills, apply them in different contexts and create an environment of excellence where people thrive, goals are achieved and organizations move towards a bright future. By mastering the art of leadership and management, we will be prepared to lead with confidence, positively influence people's lives, and drive success both professionally and personally.

1. Characteristics of a good leader

On the leadership stage, where people look to for guidance and inspiration, certain characteristics shine like beacons of excellence. A good leader is like a master of the orchestra, leading the symphony of actions, feelings and goals towards a harmonious and impactful result. It is these characteristics that outline the essence of an effective leader, creating a legacy of success, growth and transformation. In this chapter, we'll explore the map of excellence, understanding what sets a good leader apart and how these traits can be cultivated, inspiring leaders to reach their full potential.

Vision is the lodestar of leadership. A good leader has a clear and inspiring vision, a clear picture of the future he wants to create. This vision guides your decisions, motivates your team, and directs efforts toward a common goal. The ability to articulate that vision convincingly is one of the hallmarks of an inspiring leader.

Integrity is the foundation on which trust rests. A good leader is a model of honesty, ethics and respect. They act consistently, aligning their actions with their values and principles. Integrity creates an environment of trust where people feel safe knowing they are being led by someone who is truthful and trustworthy.

Empathy is the glue that holds the leader together with the team. It is the ability to understand and connect with the emotions and perspectives of others. An empathetic leader listens, understands and values individual contributions, creating an environment of respect and collaboration. Empathy strengthens the bonds between the leader and the team, inspiring a sense of unity and commitment.

Resilience is the armor that protects a leader in the face of adversity. A good leader faces challenges with determination, remaining calm even under pressure. Resilience allows the leader to lead by example, overcoming obstacles with grace and inspiring the team to do the same.

The ability to communicate effectively is an essential tool for a good leader. It is the ability to convey ideas clearly, to listen carefully and to create an open dialogue. Effective communication builds bridges of understanding, aligning the team and creating a sense of shared purpose.

By mapping the characteristics of a good leader, understanding how vision, integrity, empathy, resilience and effective communication are the traits that shape leadership excellence. We will learn to cultivate these traits, apply them in different contexts, and create a legacy of leadership that inspires, empowers, and transforms. By mastering these qualities, we will be prepared to guide with confidence, create cohesive teams and achieve extraordinary results.

2. Delegation and motivation skills

In the art of leadership, the ability to delegate and motivate is like an elegant dance, where the leader orchestrates resources, talents and energies towards a common goal. Delegating effectively is like distributing the pieces of a puzzle among the team, while motivation is the fire that ignites passion and commitment. In this chapter, we'll dive into the waters of these skills, understanding how smart delegation and genuine motivation can be the keys to achieving unimaginable levels of efficiency and achievement.

Delegation is more than simply transferring tasks. It is the art of clearly assigning responsibilities, aligned with the individual competencies of team members. A leader who masters delegation understands each person's strengths, leveraging those talents to optimize task execution and achieve goals.

By delegating, a leader also demonstrates confidence in his team. That trust is the elixir that nurtures team members' self-esteem, encouraging them to excel and take responsibility for the project's success. It encourages them to grow, develop new skills and make a significant contribution.

Motivation is like the wind under the wings of achievement. A motivating leader is one who inspires the team, who creates an environment where each person feels valued, recognized and supported in their journey. Motivation involves acknowledging achievements, encouraging in challenging times and celebrating progress.

Communication is a vital tool in motivation. A motivating leader knows how to communicate in an inspiring way, sharing the vision, recognizing effort and aligning expectations. Clear and frequent communication keeps the team engaged, aligned and excited about the work they do.

Empathy plays a key role in motivation. An empathetic leader understands the team's aspirations and concerns, adapting their approach to meet individual needs. Empathy creates an environment of support and understanding, strengthening the connection between the leader and the team.

Delegation and motivation skills, understanding how to distribute tasks intelligently, demonstrate trust in the team and create an environment of genuine motivation. We will learn to cultivate these skills, adapt them to situations, and build an environment where people flourish, contribute their full potential, and share a sense of achievement. By mastering this dance of delegation and motivation, we will be prepared to lead effective teams, achieve exceptional results and create lasting impact.

3. Decision making and problem solving

On the leadership journey, the leader is often confronted with crossroads where choices must be made and obstacles must be overcome. The ability to make wise decisions and solve complex problems is like the compass that guides the leader through the uncharted waters of challenge. These skills, intertwined, are essential to direct the team towards success, deftly overcoming obstacles and finding innovative solutions. In this chapter, we'll dive deep into the waters of decision-making and problem-solving, understanding how these competencies can shape the course of leadership and achieve remarkable results.

Decision making involves careful evaluation of options, risks, and benefits. An effective leader is able to weigh alternatives objectively, considering relevant information and varying perspectives. This ability to discern between options is critical to making choices that drive progress and achieve goals.

A wise leader also recognizes the importance of making decisions quickly, especially at crucial moments. Prolonged hesitation can lead to missed opportunities or stagnation. Reliance on intuition and the ability to act on available information are valuable attributes of a decisive leader.

Problem solving is a skill intrinsically linked to decision making. It is the ability to identify challenges, analyze their roots and create effective solutions. A problem-solving leader approaches obstacles with a creative mindset, seeing each challenge as an opportunity to grow and learn.

Collaboration plays a vital role in problem solving. A leader who values and promotes collaboration brings together the brightest minds on the team to tackle complex challenges. Diversity of perspectives and collective input can lead to innovative solutions and more effective resolutions.

Resilience is an essential quality for a leader to face the challenges that arise in decision making and problem solving. Not all decisions will be successful, not all problems will be solved in the first effort. Resilience allows the leader to face adversity with determination, learning from mistakes and seeking new approaches.

The art of decision making and problem solving, understanding how to evaluate options, act with agility, collaborate effectively and cultivate resilience. We will learn to apply these skills in different situations, overcoming obstacles and finding creative solutions. By mastering this art, we will be prepared to lead with confidence, overcome challenges with dexterity and lead the team towards remarkable results.

4. Coaching and feedback skills

On the leadership journey, the leader is not only a captain, but also a mentor, a guide who enables the team to reach its maximum potential. Coaching skills and the art of providing constructive feedback are like the tools that shape this process, allowing the leader to help individuals grow, learn, and thrive. In this chapter, we'll delve into the depth of coaching and feedback, understanding how these competencies can inspire personal development and improve team performance.

Coaching is the ability to guide, inspire and develop team skills. A leader who masters coaching identifies each member's strengths and areas of development, providing clear and constructive guidance to improve their performance. Coaching not only benefits the individual, but also strengthens the team as a whole, increasing its effectiveness.

A leader who is skilled in coaching also values continuous learning. They encourage the search for new knowledge and the development of skills, creating an environment for growth and innovation. The passion for learning infects the team, inspiring them to seek constant improvement.

Active listening is a vital coaching tool. A leader who practices active listening listens not only to the words but also to the underlying nuances, feelings, and concerns. This creates a space where people feel heard and valued, strengthening the connection between the leader and the team.

Empathy, again, plays a crucial role. An empathetic leader understands the team's individual needs, goals, and concerns. This allows the leader to adjust their coaching approach to suit each person's unique needs.

The art of providing feedback is like tuning an instrument, refining individual and collective performance. A leader who provides constructive feedback is able to convey observations clearly and respectfully, acknowledging strengths and pointing out areas for improvement. Feedback creates a learning environment, encouraging the team to seek continuous improvement.

The feedback is also bidirectional. An effective leader encourages the team to share their perspectives, ideas and concerns. This exchange of information enriches collaboration and helps identify opportunities for improvement.

Coaching skills and the art of feedback, understanding how to guide the team to success, develop a culture of learning and build an environment for growth. We will learn to apply these skills in a variety of situations, encouraging personal development and exceptional performance. By mastering these competencies, we will be prepared to guide the team with confidence, inspire the search for improvement and create a lasting impact on individual and collective growth.

5. Effective time and project management

In the whirlwind of leadership activities, effective time and project management is like a compass that keeps the leader on course, seizing every moment and steering the team toward goals. It is the ability to optimize resources, plan accurately and achieve results on time. In this chapter, we'll delve into management territory, understanding how mastery of time and effective project execution can be the pillars that underpin success, productivity, and achievement.

Effective time management is the mastery of balancing responsibilities, prioritizing tasks and avoiding the trap of procrastination. A leader who manages time skillfully is able to maximize productivity by focusing on the most impactful activities and eliminating unnecessary distractions.

Setting clear goals is a key step in time management. A leader who sets clear goals creates a compass that guides the team, directing their efforts in the right direction. These goals align with the larger vision, allowing for a focused focus and a sense of purpose.

Smart delegation also plays a vital role in effective time management. A leader who recognizes when and how to delegate leverages the team's competencies, freeing up time to focus on activities that require his personal attention. Delegation frees the leader to play a more strategic role.

The ability to prioritize is an essential tool. An effective leader knows how to identify what is urgent and important, focusing efforts where they make the most difference. Prioritization prevents wasting time on activities that do not significantly contribute to objectives.

Project management is like architecture that turns ideas into reality. It is the ability to effectively plan, execute and monitor projects. A leader who dominates project management keeps the team on track, avoiding deviations and ensuring that each step is completed within the deadlines.

Effective communication is crucial in project management. A leader who keeps the team informed, aligned, and engaged creates an environment where collaboration flourishes. Communication also allows the leader to identify any problems or challenges early, allowing corrective actions to be taken before they escalate.

The art of effective time and project management, understanding how to set goals, prioritize tasks, delegate wisely, and keep the team on track. We will learn to apply these skills in different contexts, ensuring projects are completed successfully and time is used productively. By mastering these skills, we will be prepared to lead efficiently, achieve goals and masterfully face challenges.

Chapter 5: Teamwork and Collaboration

In the tapestry of leadership, teamwork and collaboration are the threads that weave lasting connections, creating a mosaic of collective efforts in pursuit of a common goal. The leader who understands the alchemy of collaboration understands that each team member is like a unique piece of a puzzle, contributing their unique skills, perspectives, and experiences to create something greater than the sum of its parts. In this chapter, we'll delve into the depths of teamwork, unlocking the magic of collaboration and understanding how to create synergy, inspiring the team to achieve extraordinary results.

Teamwork is more than the coexistence of individuals in the same space. It is the ability to build bridges between different skills, experiences and points of view, creating an environment where diversity is valued and celebrated. A leader who fosters teamwork creates a space where people feel empowered to share, contribute, and grow together.

Collaboration is the beating heart of teamwork. It is the ability to join efforts, align goals and work towards a shared vision. A leader who promotes collaboration encourages the exchange of ideas, collective problem solving, and the creation of innovative solutions.

Communication is the pillar that sustains teamwork. A leader who promotes open and effective communication creates an environment where information flows freely, where expectations are clear, and where concerns can be expressed. Communication strengthens bonds between team members, minimizing misunderstandings and building trust.

Recognition is a powerful tool in promoting teamwork. A leader who recognizes and celebrates individual and collective contributions strengthens team motivation, reinforcing a sense of belonging and achievement. Recognition creates a virtuous cycle of engagement and dedication.

Conflict resolution is an inevitable part of teamwork. A leader who approaches conflicts constructively and equitably helps the team grow by learning to face challenges with maturity and find solutions that benefit everyone.

The dynamics of teamwork and the alchemy of collaboration, understanding how to build bridges between individual skills, foster effective communication and celebrate collective success. We will learn to apply these skills in different contexts, nurturing a culture of collaboration that leads to extraordinary results. By mastering this art, we will be prepared to lead cohesive teams, create an environment of trust and inspire the joint pursuit of ambitious goals, bringing the power of synergy to our leadership journey.

1. Building and maintaining a cohesive team

On the leadership stage, a cohesive team is like a harmonious symphony, where each member contributes their unique melody, creating a masterpiece of collaboration and excellence. Building and maintaining a cohesive team is a delicate art, which requires from the leader a deep understanding of people, culture and values that unite minds and hearts in pursuit of a shared goal. In this chapter, we'll delve into the essence of unity, understanding how to build and nurture a cohesive team that transcends challenges, celebrates successes, and builds a lasting legacy.

Building a cohesive team starts with forming a shared vision. A leader who inspires the team to embrace a clear and inspiring vision creates fertile ground for cohesion. This vision works like a beacon, guiding individual efforts towards a collective result.

Defining shared values is a solid foundation for cohesion. A leader who establishes clear values and embeds them in the cultural fabric of the team creates a sense of identity and purpose. These values shape attitudes, decisions and actions, creating a terrain where cohesion flourishes.

Leading by example is a powerful tool in building a cohesive team. A leader who embodies the values, ethics, and commitment you expect to see in the team sets the bar high. This example inspires and motivates team members to follow the same path, building cohesion from mutual respect and integrity.

Creating an environment of trust is vital for cohesion. A leader who values trust and transparency creates a space where people feel comfortable sharing ideas, voicing concerns, and seeking feedback. Trust strengthens bonds between team members, creating an environment where everyone feels valued.

Conflict management is an inevitable aspect of maintaining a cohesive team. A leader who approaches conflicts constructively, seeking solutions that benefit the team as a whole, helps to strengthen bonds and build resilience.

The celebration of collective success is like a ritual that strengthens cohesion. A leader who recognizes and celebrates milestones achieved, individual contributions and team progress creates a sense of pride and belonging, motivating the pursuit of even greater accomplishments.

The art of building and maintaining a cohesive team, understanding how to define a shared vision, establish values, lead by example, create an environment of trust and celebrate success. We will learn to apply these strategies in different contexts, nurturing a culture of cohesion that strengthens the team, overcomes challenges and generates exceptional results. By mastering this art, we will be prepared to lead cohesive teams, create an atmosphere of trust and inspire the joint pursuit of ambitious goals, building a legacy of unity and lasting success.

2. Efficient communication in teams

In the complex fabric of leadership, effective team communication is like the melody that unites each instrument, creating a symphony of understanding, alignment, and coordinated action. It is the ability to convey information clearly, to listen carefully and to cultivate an environment where the exchange of ideas is valued and respected. In this chapter, we'll delve into the universe of effective communication, understanding how mastering this art can boost collaboration, overcome obstacles, and create an environment where the team feels motivated and empowered.

Clarity is the foundation of effective communication. A leader who communicates clearly conveys information in a way that is easily understood. This avoids misunderstandings, reduces the margin for error and ensures everyone is on the same page.

Empathy is the glue that holds the team together. A leader who practices empathy when communicating understands the perspectives, concerns, and needs of each team member. This creates an environment where people feel valued and heard, strengthening the bond between the leader and the team.

Two-way communication is essential for a team to function harmoniously. A leader who encourages the team to share ideas, feedback, and concerns creates a dialogue that nurtures collaboration and innovation. Two-way communication also allows the leader to receive valuable information, identify opportunities for improvement and make informed decisions.

Effective communication also involves tailoring the message to the audience. A leader who recognizes that different team members may have different communication styles and levels of expertise adjusts their approach to meet individual needs. This ensures that the message is well received and understood by all.

Transparency is a fundamental pillar of efficient communication. A leader who values transparency shares relevant information, even if it is challenging, creating an environment of trust and engagement.

Conflict resolution through communication is a vital skill for maintaining team harmony. A leader who approaches conflict with empathy, listening to different perspectives and facilitating constructive dialogue, helps the team overcome disagreements and grow.

The symphony of effective team communication, understanding the importance of clarity, empathy, two-way communication, adaptation, transparency and conflict resolution. We will learn to apply these skills in different situations, fostering an effective communication culture that strengthens collaboration, inspires trust and maximizes the team's potential. By mastering this art, we will be prepared to lead with skill, overcome communication challenges and build an environment where the exchange of ideas and coordinated action drive success.

3. Dealing with conflicts and disagreements

In the intricate fabric of leadership, conflict and disagreement are like the cornerstones of evolution. Every divergent perspective, every disagreement, offers the opportunity for growth, learning, and innovation. The ability to handle these moments is key to keeping the team in balance, resolving differences constructively, and creating an environment where disagreement is seen as a path to excellence. In this chapter, we'll explore strategies for reconciling conflict and disagreement, understanding how to turn challenges into opportunities and cultivate fertile ground for collaboration.

Understanding the nature of conflicts is the starting point. A leader who recognizes that conflicts are a natural part of team dynamics embraces this reality with maturity. This allows you to fearlessly approach conflicts, viewing them as learning and growth points.

Effective communication plays a vital role in conflict resolution. A leader who promotes open dialogue, encourages the expression of different perspectives, and seeks to understand the root causes of conflicts creates an environment where resolution is more accessible.

Empathy is a powerful tool for dealing with conflict. An empathetic leader understands the emotions, concerns, and motivations of each party involved, making it easier to build bridges and find solutions that benefit everyone.

Negotiation is an essential skill for resolving disagreements. A leader who masters the art of negotiation seeks compromise solutions that take into account the needs of all parties. This creates an environment for cooperation and joint construction of solutions.

Mediation is a valuable tool in conflicts that cannot be resolved directly. A leader who acts as a mediator helps the parties to find common ground, understand each other's perspectives, and work together to resolve the conflict.

Constructive conflict resolution is a journey, not a final destination. A leader who recognizes that some conflicts may take time to fully resolve maintains an ongoing commitment to open communication, empathy, and finding solutions that benefit the team as a whole.

Strategies to deal with conflicts and disagreements, understanding the importance of communication, empathy, negotiation and mediation. We will learn to apply these strategies in different contexts, transforming conflicts into opportunities for growth and collaboration. By mastering this skill, we will be prepared to lead with balance, overcome challenges and create an environment where diversity of thought is valued, and disagreement is seen as a catalyst for innovation and excellence.

4. Fostering collaboration and creativity

On the path of leadership, collaboration and creativity are the driving forces that drive the team towards innovation, overcoming challenges and achieving remarkable results.

Cultivating an environment where these qualities flourish is the hallmark of a visionary leader, who understands that the team's true potential is unlocked when minds unite, ideas intertwine, and the pursuit of innovative solutions is encouraged. In this chapter, we'll delve into the art of fostering collaboration and creativity, understanding how to create fertile ground where diversity of thought is valued, barriers are broken down, and the search for innovative solutions is a shared journey.

Fostering a collaborative environment starts with leading by example. A leader who values collaboration in his actions, who seeks input from others, and who recognizes individual contributions creates a pattern that inspires the team. This example demonstrates that collaboration is valued and encouraged.

Creating spaces for the exchange of ideas is a powerful strategy. A leader who encourages brainstorming sessions, discussion forums, and collaborative workgroups opens the door for creativity to flourish. These spaces provide a terrain where minds can connect, perspectives intersect and new ideas emerge.

Valuing diversity of thought is essential. A leader who recognizes that different points of view bring richness to the team creates an environment where innovation is nurtured. Diversity of thought encourages creativity, leading to more robust solutions and a culture of continuous learning.

Promoting open and respectful communication is a cornerstone of collaboration and creativity. A leader who encourages the expression of ideas, who values respect for differing perspectives, and who creates an environment where everyone feels comfortable sharing builds a healthy collaboration space.

The celebration of creativity and collaborative effort is a tool that reinforces these qualities. A leader who recognizes and celebrates innovations, creative solutions, and team contributions nurtures a sense of pride and inspiration.

Strategies to foster collaboration and creativity, understanding the importance of example, creating spaces for the exchange of ideas, valuing diversity of thought, respectful communication and celebration. We will learn to apply these strategies in different contexts, creating an environment where innovation flourishes, challenges are creatively faced and the joint search for exceptional solutions is the norm. By mastering this art, we will be prepared to lead with vision, cultivate an environment of collaboration and creativity, and inspire the team to reach new heights of excellence and achievement.

5. Alignment of objectives and goals in the team

In the leadership journey, the alignment of objectives and goals is like the map that guides the team towards the desired destination. Each team member needs to have a clear understanding of what is being pursued, how their contributions fit into the bigger picture, and what their role is in achieving the collective goals. The leader who masters the art of alignment creates a symphony of coordinated efforts, optimizing resources, minimizing deviations, and building a path that leads to the achievement of goals. In this chapter, we'll enter the world of aligning goals and objectives, understanding how to create a shared vision, communicate clearly, and ensure that everyone on the team is pulling in the same direction.

Defining a shared vision is the starting point. A leader who inspires the team to embrace a clear and ambitious vision creates direction for the journey. This vision connects individual goals to collective goals, establishing a common purpose that guides each step.

Clear and frequent communication is the key to alignment. A leader who communicates the objectives, goals, and relevance of each part in the big picture keeps everyone on the team informed and engaged. Communication avoids misunderstandings, reduces uncertainty, and strengthens the connection between the leader and the team.

Setting clear goals is an essential step in alignment. A leader who sets specific, measurable, achievable, relevant, and time-bound goals (SMART) creates a framework that allows the team to understand what needs to be achieved and how success will be measured.

Smart delegation is a tool that connects collective goals to individual tasks. A leader who distributes tasks aligned with the competencies of each team member and who monitors progress ensures that alignment is not lost on a day-to-day basis.

Feedback is a strategy that keeps the alignment in constant adjustment. A leader who provides constructive feedback, recognizing contributions and offering guidance for improvement, ensures the team stays on track.

Reviewing and adjusting goals is an ongoing practice. A leader who measures progress, celebrates achievements, learns from challenges, and makes necessary adjustments ensures alignment is dynamic and adaptable.

Strategies for aligning objectives and goals, understanding the importance of a shared vision, clear communication, goal setting SMART , smart delegation, feedback, and continual review. We will learn to apply these strategies in different contexts, ensuring that the team remains on the road to success, with each member understanding their role and contributing to the achievement of collective goals. By mastering this art, we will be prepared to lead with clarity, create an environment of engagement and achievement, and achieve results that reflect the union of efforts towards a shared vision.

Chapter 6: Adaptability and Flexibility

In the dynamic dance of leadership, adaptability and flexibility are like the wings that allow the leader to navigate through change, overcome unforeseen challenges, and evolve in an ever-changing world. These are the skills that allow you to adjust your trajectory without losing your way, embrace new opportunities and firmly guide the team even in the face of uncertainty. In this chapter, we'll explore the power of resilience, understanding how adaptability and flexibility are key tools for leading in times of change, fostering a culture of continuous learning, and keeping the team moving, no matter what winds blow.

Adaptability is the ability to adjust to changes effectively. An adaptable leader is like a conductor conducting a symphony, adjusting to the rhythm and melody of the environment, while keeping the vision clear and inspiring the team to evolve together.

Flexibility is the ability to keep an open mind and a willingness to change course when necessary. A flexible leader does not see deviations as obstacles, but as opportunities for growth and learning. This flexibility allows exploration of new approaches, adaptation to new circumstances and the ability to deal with the unexpected.

Transparent communication is a vital element of adaptability and flexibility. A leader who clearly communicates the reasons for changes and shares relevant information helps the team understand and accept the need to adapt. This creates an environment where resilience builds, and the team meets challenges head-on.

Leading by example is a strategy that inspires adaptability. A leader who demonstrates a willingness to embrace change, learn from mistakes, and adapt to new demands models resilience for the team. This example creates fertile ground for a culture of adaptability and flexibility.

Creative problem solving is a tool that amplifies adaptability. A leader who encourages the team to think creatively, seek innovative solutions and adapt to ever-evolving challenges builds a resilient team, capable of facing any situation.

In the power of resilience, understanding the importance of adaptability and flexibility in leadership. We will learn to apply these skills in different contexts, cultivating a culture of continuous learning and keeping the team moving, no matter the circumstances. By mastering this art, we will be prepared to lead with resilience, face changes with confidence and inspire the team to embrace constant evolution, achieving remarkable results, even in the most challenging situations.

1. Dealing with change and uncertainty

In the winding path of leadership, the scenery is often full of unexpected curves and hazy horizons. Dealing with change and uncertainty is like navigating turbulent seas, requiring leadership, courage, and adaptation skills from leaders. It is the ability to keep the team together, to face challenges with resilience and to guide with confidence even when the path is uncertain. In this chapter, we'll explore the skills needed to navigate change and uncertainty, understanding how a leader can be the compass that keeps the team on course, even when the waters are rough.

Understanding the nature of the changes is the starting point. A leader who recognizes that changes are part of the journey, that they are opportunities for growth and that they can bring improvements, faces challenges with a positive mindset. This perspective creates fertile ground for resilience and adaptation.

Transparent communication is a vital tool for dealing with change and uncertainty. A leader who keeps the team informed about changes, shares the reasons behind decisions, and provides a clear vision of the future helps to reduce anxiety and uncertainty.

Empathy is an essential quality when dealing with change. An empathetic leader understands the concerns, fears and needs of the team, creating an environment where feelings are respected. This empathy strengthens the connection between the leader and the team, and allows everyone to feel heard and supported.

The ability to lead by example is an important pillar. A leader who demonstrates resilience, adapting to change with courage and facing uncertainty with determination, inspires the team to do the same. This example creates a sense of confidence and guidance, even in the most challenging times.

Expectation management is a valuable strategy. A leader who communicates realities, challenges and possible scenarios helps the team understand the possibilities and be prepared for different outcomes. This avoids unpleasant surprises and keeps the team in a state of readiness.

The skills to deal with change and uncertainty, understanding the importance of understanding change, transparent communication, empathy, example, and managing expectations. We will learn to apply these skills in different contexts, keeping the team motivated, confident and resilient, even when the challenges are great and the future is uncertain. By mastering this art, we will be prepared to lead with courage, face changes with determination and guide the team through the turbulent waters, towards a future full of possibilities.

2. Continuous learning and personal development

On the perpetual journey of leadership, continuous learning and personal development are like the fuel that propels the leader to new horizons, to improve his skills and to become the best version of himself. It is the relentless pursuit of knowledge, the willingness to evolve and the pursuit of growth opportunities that distinguish exceptional leaders. In this chapter, we'll explore the importance of continuous learning and personal development, understanding how leadership is a journey of constant improvement that not only benefits the leader, but also the team and the organization as a whole.

The pursuit of knowledge is the foundation of continuous learning. A leader who values education, reads, researches, attends courses and seeks to stay current on relevant trends in the field, enriches his knowledge base and enhances his ability to make informed decisions.

Self-criticism is a powerful tool for personal development. A leader who evaluates his actions and results, identifies areas for improvement, and is willing to acknowledge his shortcomings creates a growth mindset that inspires the team to do the same.

Constructive feedback is a valuable source of learning. A leader who seeks feedback, listens humbly, and seizes opportunities for improvement demonstrates that he or she is committed to growing and providing an environment where learning is valued.

Balanced self-confidence is a quality that drives personal development. A leader who believes in his abilities, seeks challenges and is willing to step out of his comfort zone creates an environment where the team is encouraged to seek personal growth.

The ability to teach and guide is a manifestation of continuous learning. A leader who shares knowledge, guides the team and promotes a mutual learning environment strengthens the culture of growth in the organization.

The importance of continuous learning and personal development, including the search for knowledge, self-criticism, constructive feedback, balanced self-confidence and the ability to teach and guide. We will learn to apply these principles in leadership, creating an environment where learning is a fundamental value, where personal growth is encouraged and where the constant search for improvement is a central characteristic. By mastering this approach, we will be prepared to lead with excellence, constantly evolve and inspire the team to achieve remarkable results, while growing and developing personally.

3. Resilience and overcoming obstacles

On the steep path of leadership, resilience and the ability to overcome obstacles are like the deep roots that keep the leader firm in the midst of storms. These are the skills that allow you to face adversity with determination, turn challenges into opportunities and keep moving forward, even when the path is difficult. Resilience is the quality that allows the leader to rise after falls, learn from difficulties and inspire the team to persist. In this chapter, we'll delve into the art of resilience and overcoming obstacles, understanding how to cultivate the inner strength needed to weather storms, turn obstacles into stepping stones, and guide your team confidently toward success, no matter what the circumstances.

Resilience starts with mindset. A resilient leader sees adversity as an opportunity for growth, believes he can overcome obstacles and maintains a clear vision, even in difficult times. This mindset creates a solid foundation that allows the leader to maintain composure in the face of challenges.

Emotional management is an essential skill for resilience. A leader who understands his emotions, who knows how to handle stress, and who maintains balance even in intense situations inspires the team to do the same. Emotional management strengthens the connection between the leader and the team, creating an environment where everyone is mutually supportive.

Creative problem solving is a tool that drives overcoming obstacles. A leader who encourages the team to find innovative solutions, think creatively and approach problems strategically creates an environment where challenges are turned into opportunities for learning and growth.

Leading by example is a pillar of resilience. A leader who faces obstacles with courage, who is undeterred by difficulties and who demonstrates a positive attitude, inspires the team to do the same. This example creates an environment where resilience is valued and cultivated.

Celebrating small victories is a strategy that strengthens resilience. A leader who recognizes and celebrates progress, even when goals haven't been fully achieved, keeps team motivation high and creates a sense of accomplishment.

The art of resilience and overcoming obstacles, understanding the importance of mindset, emotional management, creative problem solving, leading by example and celebrating victories. We will learn to apply these skills in different contexts, cultivating a culture of resilience, resilience and growth, where adversity is seen as an opportunity to evolve and achieve remarkable results. By mastering this approach, we will be prepared to lead with determination, face challenges with confidence and guide the team through adversity, towards a future full of achievements.

4. Seeking opportunities in times of crisis

In the journey of leadership, moments of crisis are like the dark nights that often provide us with the brightest opportunities. It is in these moments that the leader's vision is tested, his ability to identify gaps and his ability to guide the team through the storms is revealed. The crisis, far from being an insurmountable obstacle, can be an unexpected source of growth, innovation and renewal. In this chapter, we'll explore how to look for opportunities in the midst of crisis, understanding how the leader can be the light that illuminates the way, identifying positive perspectives and guiding the team toward success, even when the clouds are thickest.

The opportunity mindset is the starting point. A leader who keeps an open mind, who looks for valuable lessons in the midst of crisis and who believes that it is possible to find opportunities even in the most challenging situations creates a fertile ground for innovation.

Active search for solutions is a crucial skill in times of crisis. A leader who encourages the team to think creatively, to look for alternatives and to explore new paths turns the crisis into an opportunity to reinvent processes, products and strategies.

The ability to adapt is a foundation for seeking opportunities in times of crisis. A leader who is willing to adjust course, change strategy, and adapt to changing circumstances demonstrates that he is alert to opportunities that may arise, even in challenging situations.

Leading by example is a powerful strategy. A leader who stays calm in the midst of crisis, who maintains a positive attitude and who looks for opportunities inspires the team to do the same. This example creates an environment where resilience is valued and the pursuit of opportunities is a shared attitude.

Clear communication is essential to identify opportunities in times of crisis. A leader who openly communicates the situation, the actions taken and the possible opportunities that may arise keeps the team informed and engaged in the search for solutions.

The search for opportunities in times of crisis, understanding the importance of the opportunity mentality, the active search for solutions, adaptability, leadership by example and clear communication. We will learn to apply these strategies in different contexts, transforming the crisis into an opportunity for growth, innovation and renewal. By mastering this approach, we will be prepared to lead with vision, identify opportunities even in the most challenging situations and guide the team towards success, even when the clouds are darkest.

5. How to stay current in an ever-changing world

In the age of information and speed, the leader who wants to stand out needs to be an agile navigator, constantly adjusting the sails to keep up with changes in the scenario. In a world where evolution is the norm and new trends emerge quickly, the quest for knowledge and continual adaptation are essential to effective leadership. In this chapter, we'll explore practical strategies for staying current in an ever-changing world, understanding how to become an informed leader who can anticipate trends, and how to build a culture of constant learning on your team.

The active search for information is the starting point. A leader who seeks out credible news sources, reads regularly about her field, and is aware of emerging trends is better equipped to make informed decisions and lead wisely.

Networking is a valuable tool for keeping up to date. A leader who cultivates professional relationships, participates in focus groups, and is involved in events relevant to his field, expands his vision and has access to valuable insights.

Ongoing training is essential. A leader who invests in his own development, attends courses, workshops and conferences, keeps his skills up to date and is willing to learn from the best maintains a competitive edge.

Leading by example is a pillar. A leader who demonstrates the value of continuous learning, who encourages the team to stay current and who values the pursuit of knowledge, creates a culture of constant learning, which becomes a driving force for innovation.

Adaptability is an essential skill. A leader who is willing to adjust his strategies, embrace new technologies and take innovative approaches stays relevant in an ever-evolving world.

The search for constant updating, understanding the importance of the active search for information, the network of contacts, continuous training, leadership by example and the ability to adapt. We will learn to apply these strategies in different contexts, building a solid foundation to stay current, to lead with excellence and to guide the team in an ever-changing world. By mastering this approach, we will be prepared to lead with vision, adapt to new realities and be at the forefront of trends, ensuring that our journey is marked by excellence and innovation.

Chapter 7: Critical Thinking and Problem Solving

In the complex dance of leadership, critical thinking and problem-solving skills are like the precise cogs that turn the larger cog of strategy. They are the capabilities that allow the leader to analyze information, identify opportunities, make informed decisions and face challenges effectively. In this chapter, we'll explore the art of critical thinking and problem-solving mastery, understanding how leadership transcends the surface, delving into deep analysis, strategic creativity, and solving complex issues.

Critical thinking is the foundation of informed leadership. A leader who questions, evaluates evidence, considers multiple perspectives, and rigorously analyzes information is better equipped to make sound decisions and lead with confidence.

Strategic creativity is a valuable tool in problem solving. A leader who seeks innovative approaches, who encourages the team to think "outside the box" and who looks for solutions that go beyond the obvious, finds unique ways to overcome obstacles.

Making informed decisions is a cornerstone of critical thinking. A leader who carefully evaluates the available options, weighs the consequences, and chooses the course of action that most aligns with the goals of the team and the organization makes decisions that are sound and well-founded.

The ability to solve complex problems is a manifestation of critical thinking. A leader who tackles intricate challenges, who breaks problems down into manageable components, and who guides the team through obstacles with resilience and determination demonstrates the ability to lead effectively in challenging environments.

Clear communication is essential for problem solving and critical thinking. A leader who articulates reasoning, shares detailed analysis, and explains the decision-making process creates an environment where the team understands the "why" behind actions, fostering a sense of clarity and engagement.

The art of critical thinking and mastery of problem solving, understanding the importance of critical thinking, strategic creativity, informed decision making, complex problem solving skills and clear communication. We will learn to apply these skills in different contexts, improving our ability to lead effectively, face challenges with confidence and guide the team with clarity and resilience. By mastering this approach, we will be prepared to lead with excellence, find innovative solutions and skillfully overcome obstacles, making our journey as leaders a path marked by notable achievements.

1. Developing analytical skills

In the complex symphony of leadership, developing analytical skills is like the fine tuning that allows a leader to pick up on nuances, understand hidden patterns, and make informed decisions. These skills are like a telescope that allows us to see beyond the surface, diving into the deepest layers of data, information and situations. In this chapter, we'll explore the importance of developing analytical skills in leadership, understanding how the ability to critically analyze information, identify trends, and translate data into strategic actions is a critical differentiator for success as a leader.

Critical analysis is the foundation of analytical skills. A leader who questions, evaluates, and challenges available information develops a perspective that allows identifying significant details and understanding different perspectives.

The ability to identify patterns is an essential element. A leader who recognizes emerging trends, correlations, and cause-and-effect relationships is better equipped to anticipate future scenarios and make informed decisions.

Data interpretation is a cornerstone of analytical skills. A leader who knows how to turn information into valuable insights, who understands the meaning behind the numbers and who can clearly communicate those insights to the team is able to guide the group towards goals and objectives.

Evidence-based decision-making is a manifestation of analytical skills. A leader who uses hard data, analysis, and information as the foundation of his decisions creates a leadership environment that values informed thinking and inspires the team to take that approach.

Leading by example is a driving factor. A leader who demonstrates the importance of analytical skills, who encourages the team to develop them, and who values critical and reasoned thinking creates an environment where the pursuit of analysis is a shared characteristic.

The development of analytical skills, understanding the importance of critical analysis, identifying patterns, interpreting data, evidence-based decision-making and leading by example. We will learn to apply these skills in different contexts, improving our ability to lead with reason, understand trends and translate information into strategic actions. By mastering this approach, we will be prepared to lead with insight, make informed decisions and guide the team on a journey of success, based on informed analysis and clear perspectives.

2. Systematic approach to solving problems

In the intricate tapestry of leadership, a systematic approach to problem solving is like the common thread that holds all the pieces together. It is the method that allows the leader to approach challenges in an organized way, disassemble complex problems into manageable steps and make informed decisions. In this chapter, we'll explore the importance of a systematic approach to solving problems in leadership, understanding how the structure, detailed analysis, and effectiveness of the problem-solving process are essential to achieving consistent results and guiding the team toward success.

A clear definition of the problem is the starting point. A leader who understands the nature of the challenge, identifies its root causes, and sets clear goals for resolution is better equipped to lead the team toward solutions.

Careful analysis is an essential step. A leader who collects relevant information, examines data and considers multiple perspectives on the problem is able to identify the best approaches and make informed decisions.

Breaking the problem down into manageable steps is a cornerstone of the systematic approach. A leader who breaks the problem down into smaller components, creates an action plan, and assigns responsibilities for each step in the process allows the team to approach the problem in an organized and effective way.

Constant evaluation is a crucial strategy. A leader who monitors progress, reviews results, and makes adjustments when necessary ensures that the problem-solving process is adaptive and geared toward success.

Effective communication is a tool that keeps everyone on the same page. A leader who keeps the team informed about progress, challenges faced and actions to be taken creates a collaborative environment where everyone is involved in finding solutions.

A systematic approach to problem solving, understanding the importance of clear problem definition, detailed analysis, breaking the problem into manageable steps, constant evaluation, and effective communication. We will learn to apply this approach in different contexts, improving our ability to lead with organization, solve problems in a structured way and effectively guide the team towards overcoming challenges. By mastering this approach, we will be prepared to lead with precision, make informed decisions and confidently lead the team towards remarkable results.

3. Data-based decision-making

In the complex landscape of leadership, data-driven decision making is like the reliable compass that guides the leader through the tumultuous waters of the business world. It's the approach that allows leaders to use solid information to guide choices, assess scenarios, and chart an informed path to success. In this chapter, we'll explore the importance of data-driven decision making in leadership, understanding how objective analysis, the search for reliable information, and the judicious use of data are essential elements for leading effectively in a dynamic environment.

Collecting reliable data is the starting point. A leader who seeks solid information, uses reliable sources, and understands the importance of accurate data is in a position to make informed decisions.

Objective analysis is a crucial skill. A leader who evaluates data impartially, considers multiple perspectives, and weighs hard evidence has the ability to identify the best approaches and minimize the impact of personal bias.

Translating data into valuable insights is a cornerstone of data-driven decision making. A leader who understands the meaning behind the numbers, who extrapolates trends and who clearly communicates insights to the team is able to lead based on objective information.

Transparent communication about data is an essential strategy. A leader who shares relevant information with the team, who explains the reasoning behind decisions, and who promotes transparency creates a leadership environment where the pursuit of data is valued and shared.

The active pursuit of continuous learning in data analysis is a manifestation of leading by example. A leader who demonstrates the importance of data-driven decision-making, who encourages the team to seek objective information, and who values informed analysis creates a culture where the pursuit of data is a shared characteristic.

Data-driven decision making, understanding the importance of collecting reliable data, objective analysis, translating data into valuable insights, transparently communicating about data, and actively pursuing continuous learning. We will learn to apply this approach in different contexts, improving our ability to lead with objective information, evaluate scenarios in an informed way and confidently guide the team towards solid results. By mastering this approach, we will be prepared to lead clearly, make informed decisions and lead the team with determination, making our leadership journey a path marked by consistent successes.

4. Creative and innovative thinking

In the journey of leadership, creative and innovative thinking is like the flame that illuminates new paths and opens doors to the future. It is the capacity that allows the leader to see beyond the conventional, generate original solutions and inspire the team to explore unexplored territories. In this chapter, we'll explore the importance of creative and innovative thinking in leadership, understanding how an open mind, seeking out unique approaches, and fostering an environment of innovation are key to leading with excellence in an ever-evolving world.

An open mind is the starting point for creative thinking. A leader who welcomes new ideas, considers diverse perspectives, and is willing to question the status quo creates fertile ground for innovation.

The search for inspiration is a valuable practice. A leader who looks for references, explores different areas of knowledge and encourages the team to seek inspiration from different sources broadens the creative horizon, generating richer and more innovative solutions.

The creation of an environment of innovation is a fundamental strategy. A leader who encourages creative thinking, values experimentation, and allows the team to take risks in search of original solutions creates a space where innovation flourishes.

The connection of ideas is a pillar of creative and innovative thinking. A leader who encourages collaboration, promotes the exchange of ideas and brings the team together to explore different perspectives enhances collective creativity, generating unique solutions.

Leading by example is a motivating factor. A leader who demonstrates the importance of creative and innovative thinking, who encourages the team to think "outside the box" and who values original approaches creates a culture of innovation that is reflected in all aspects of the journey.

Creative and innovative thinking in leadership, understanding the importance of an open mind, seeking inspiration, creating an environment of innovation, connecting ideas and leading by example. We will learn to apply this approach in different contexts, improving our ability to lead creatively, generate innovative solutions and inspire the team to explore new horizons. By mastering this approach, we will be prepared to lead with vision, drive innovation and lead the team towards remarkable achievements, marking our journey as leaders with a stamp of originality and success.

5. Improving your ability to solve complex challenges

In the tapestry of leadership, the ability to solve complex challenges is like the sharp needle that sews together each thread, uniting strategy and execution. It is the competence that allows the leader to face intricate obstacles, analyze multifaceted situations and guide the team towards solid results. In this chapter, we'll explore the importance of improving your ability to solve complex problems in leadership, understanding how deep analysis, resilience in the face of complexity, and a structured approach are essential to leading with excellence in a challenging environment.

Deep analytics is the foundation for solving complex challenges. A leader who dives into the nuances of the problem, understands its ramifications, and considers multiple variables is better equipped to make informed decisions.

Resilience in the face of complexity is a crucial element. A leader who tackles intricate obstacles with determination, who doesn't waver in the face of challenging scenarios, and who confidently guides the team through complexity demonstrates the ability to lead effectively.

The structured approach is a cornerstone of complex problem solving. A leader who breaks the challenge down into manageable chunks, creates a clear plan of action, and guides the team through well-defined steps allows complexity to be tackled in an organized way.

The search for continuous learning in problem solving is a manifestation of leadership by example. A leader who demonstrates the importance of resolving complex challenges, who encourages the team to approach obstacles with structure, and who values the resolute approach creates a leadership environment where the pursuit of effective resolutions is a shared characteristic.

Improve your ability to solve complex challenges by understanding the importance of deep analysis, resilience in the face of complexity, a structured approach and leading by example. We will learn to apply this approach in different contexts, improving our ability to lead with resolve, face challenges with confidence and guide the team towards solid solutions. By mastering this perspective, we will be prepared to lead with dexterity, overcome complex obstacles and lead the team on a successful journey, marked by notable achievements even in challenging environments.

Chapter 8: Interpersonal Communication

In the leadership journey, interpersonal communication is like the bridge that connects leaders and teams, translating visions into actions and strengthening the relationship between all those involved. It is the skill that allows the leader to convey clarity, listen with empathy and inspire confidence, making collaboration fluid and effective. In this chapter, we'll explore the importance of interpersonal communication in leadership, understanding how active listening, clear expression, relationship building, and communication skills are key to leading with excellence in an interconnected environment.

Active listening is the starting point. A leader who listens carefully, understands the team's perspectives, and is willing to receive feedback creates an environment where communication flows naturally, fostering a sense of appreciation and mutual respect.

Clear expression is a valuable tool. A leader who communicates his ideas clearly, uses concrete examples and communicates information in an accessible way inspires confidence and avoids misunderstandings, ensuring that the vision is understood by all.

Building relationships is a cornerstone of interpersonal communication. A leader who makes genuine connections, encourages teamwork, and fosters an environment where everyone feels valued strengthens team engagement, making it easier to collaborate and achieve goals.

Communication skills are a manifestation of leading by example. A leader who demonstrates the importance of interpersonal communication, who encourages the team to communicate effectively, and who values respectful and open expression creates a culture where communication is a shared characteristic.

Interpersonal communication in leadership, understanding the importance of active listening, clear expression, relationship building and communication skills. We will learn to apply this approach in different contexts, improving our ability to lead with empathy, convey information clearly and build an environment where communication is effective and valued. By mastering this perspective, we will be prepared to lead fluidly, strengthen interpersonal relationships and successfully lead the team towards remarkable results.

1. Building professional relationships

In the complex web of leadership, the ability to build solid professional relationships is like the foundation that sustains growth and collaboration. It is the competence that allows the leader to establish authentic connections, cultivate strategic partnerships and strengthen trust inside and outside the team. In this chapter, we'll explore the importance of building professional relationships in leadership, understanding how empathy, effective communication, collaboration, and networking are key to leading with excellence in an interdependent environment.

Empathy is the starting point. A leader who understands the needs, feelings, and perspectives of the team and co-workers creates an environment where trust and respect flourish, facilitating collaboration and the sharing of ideas.

Effective communication is a valuable tool. A leader who communicates clearly, listens carefully, and is willing to express ideas respectfully lays a solid foundation for healthy professional relationships.

Collaboration is a pillar of building relationships. A leader who encourages teamwork, recognizes everyone's contributions, and fosters an environment where people feel valued strengthens the team's sense of belonging and cohesion.

Building a network of contacts is a crucial strategy. A leader who cultivates relationships in his area of expertise, seeks to learn from other professionals and shares knowledge creates an environment where the exchange of experiences and continuous learning are valued.

Leading by example is a driving factor. A leader who demonstrates the importance of building professional relationships, who encourages the team to make connections, and who values empathy, communication, and collaboration creates a culture where building relationships is a shared trait.

Building professional relationships in leadership, understanding the importance of empathy, effective communication, collaboration and building a network of contacts. We will learn to apply this approach in different contexts, improving our ability to lead with authenticity, build trust and lead the team successfully in building solid professional relationships. By mastering this perspective, we will be prepared to lead with meaningful connections, foster strategic partnerships and lead the team towards a cohesive and collaborative work environment.

2. Assertive and constructive communication

In the leadership journey, assertive and constructive communication is like a valuable tool that helps build bridges, eliminate misunderstandings and strengthen team growth. It is the skill that allows the leader to express his ideas clearly, deal with challenging situations constructively and promote an environment where everyone feels valued. In this chapter, we will explore the importance of assertive and constructive communication in leadership, understanding how direct expression, constructive feedback, conflict resolution and the promotion of an open dialogue are fundamental to leading with excellence in an interdependent environment.

Direct expression is like a well-marked road. A leader who communicates his ideas clearly, directly and respectfully avoids misunderstandings, which is essential to ensure the team is aligned with goals and purpose.

Constructive feedback is a tool that helps the team grow. A leader who offers feedback in a constructive way, points out strengths and opportunities for improvement, creates a continuous learning environment where everyone can improve their skills.

Conflict resolution is a pillar of constructive communication. A leader who approaches conflicts objectively, encourages collaboration and promotes solutions, helps the team overcome obstacles, which is essential to maintain a harmonious work environment.

Promoting open dialogue is like opening windows in a stuffy room. A leader who encourages the team to share ideas, listen to different perspectives and openly discuss relevant issues encourages creativity and innovation, which is vital for team growth.

Leading by example is an inspirational factor. A leader who demonstrates the importance of assertive and constructive communication, who values clear expression, constructive feedback and open dialogue, creates a culture where communication is respectful and valued by all.

Assertive and constructive communication in leadership, understanding the importance of direct expression, constructive feedback, conflict resolution and the promotion of an open dialogue. We will learn to apply this approach in different contexts, improving our ability to lead clearly, handle challenges constructively and create an environment where communication is effective and valued. By mastering this perspective, we will be prepared to lead with impact, promote healthy relationships and successfully lead the team in pursuit of remarkable results.

3. Effective and constructive feedback

On the leadership journey, mastering the skill of giving effective and constructive feedback is like tuning a musical instrument to the perfect melody. It is the competence that allows the leader to provide clear guidelines, recognize work well done and promote the continuous development of the team. In this chapter, we'll explore the importance of effective and constructive feedback in leadership, understanding how clear delivery, sincere recognition, encouraging growth, and setting goals are critical to leading with excellence in a learning and evolving environment.

Clear delivery of feedback is like a compass that guides the team. A leader who accurately communicates observations, focusing on specific behaviors, facilitates understanding and makes feedback more valuable for development.

Sincere recognition is a powerful motivational tool. A leader who values the team's efforts, celebrates achievements and genuinely expresses gratitude, strengthens engagement, encouraging everyone to continue to give their best.

Encouraging growth is a cornerstone of constructive feedback. A leader who identifies opportunities for improvement, offers constructive suggestions and supports the team in its evolution, contributes to individual and collective development, resulting in a more skilled and prepared team.

Setting goals is like charting a roadmap for the future. A leader who sets clear goals, guides the team in the right direction and sets realistic expectations, creates a sense of purpose, driving everyone towards success.

Leading by example is inspiring. A leader who demonstrates the importance of effective and constructive feedback, who values team development, the celebration of achievements and constant learning, creates a culture where feedback is a fundamental part of the process of growth and evolution.

The art of effective and constructive feedback in leadership, understanding the importance of clear delivery, sincere recognition, encouraging growth and goal setting. We will learn to apply this approach in different contexts, improving our ability to lead with guidance, value evolution and lead the team to a level of excellence, where continuous growth is a distinctive mark. By mastering this perspective, we will be prepared to lead with impact, encourage individual and collective development, and seek remarkable results in an environment of constant learning.

4. Understanding the needs of others

In the leadership orchestra, the ability to understand the needs of others is like the melody that harmonizes relationships and creates an environment of collaboration. It is the competence that allows the leader to connect with his team, identify what is important to each individual and meet his aspirations and challenges. In this chapter, we will explore the importance of tuning in to empathy in leadership, understanding how active listening, recognizing talent, creating a supportive environment, and adapting to needs are key to leading with excellence in an environment of diversity and mutual growth.

Active listening is like opening a door to the hearts of others. A leader who listens carefully, welcomes concerns, and understands the team's perspectives creates an environment where everyone feels valued, fostering a sense of belonging and openness.

Talent recognition is a source of inspiration. A leader who identifies each team member's strengths, values individual contributions, and creates opportunities for those talents to shine, fosters an environment where motivation and trust grow.

Creating a supportive environment is a cornerstone of empathetic leadership. A leader who offers support, encourages professional development and cares about the well-being of the team strengthens commitment and the ability to overcome challenges.

Adapting to needs is like adjusting a lens to see clearly. A leader who understands that different people have different needs, adapts his approach to leadership, offering personalized support, promoting an environment of mutual respect.

Leading by example is the foundation for empathetic leadership. A leader who demonstrates the importance of understanding the needs of others, who encourages the team to listen, value talents and support each other, creates a culture where empathy is a shared characteristic.

Empathy in leadership, understanding the importance of active listening, recognizing talent, creating a supportive environment and adapting to needs. We will learn to apply this approach in different contexts, improving our ability to lead with sensitivity, value individualities and lead the team to an environment where everyone feels understood and supported. By mastering this perspective, we will be prepared to lead with impact, promote healthy relationships and lead the team towards remarkable results, where collaboration and well-being are fundamental pillars.

5. Development of networking and connections

On the leadership journey, developing networking and connections is like weaving a web of relationships that expands horizons and opens doors to opportunities. It is the competence that allows the leader to establish professional ties, build a solid network of contacts and promote synergies that drive growth. In this chapter, we will explore the importance of developing networks and connections in leadership, understanding how building relationships, seeking continuous learning, strategic collaboration and contributing to the community are fundamental to leading with excellence in an interconnected environment and in constant evolution.

Building relationships is like planting seeds in fertile soil. A leader who makes genuine connections, values a diversity of perspectives, and cultivates professional friendships creates a solid foundation for future opportunities.

The pursuit of continuous learning is a source of growth. A leader who seeks to expand his knowledge, learn from other professionals and share experiences, expands his possibilities and keeps up to date in a world in constant change.

Strategic collaboration is a pillar of networking development. A leader who pursues strategic partnerships, identifies collaboration opportunities, and builds valuable alliances strengthens his or her network, which is essential to achieving ambitious goals.

Contributing to the community is a form of mutual enrichment. A leader who shares knowledge, supports relevant initiatives and contributes to the growth of the community creates an environment of trust and appreciation, where the return is shared by all.

Leading by example is an inspiration for building networks. A leader who demonstrates the importance of networking, who encourages the team to make connections and who values collaboration, creates a culture where networking is seen as a valuable strategy.

Building networks and connections in leadership, understanding the importance of building relationships, seeking continuous learning, strategic collaboration and contributing to the community. We will learn to apply this approach in different contexts, improving our ability to lead with a strategic vision, seize opportunities for growth and lead the team towards a rich and valuable network of contacts. By mastering this perspective, we will be prepared to lead with impact, establish meaningful professional ties and seek remarkable results through strategic connections.

Chapter 9: Professional Etiquette and Empathy

In the world of leadership, knowing and applying professional etiquette is like skillfully navigating a sea of relationships and interactions. It is the compass that guides us towards appropriate behaviours, cultural sensitivity and, above all, genuine empathy. In this chapter, we'll explore how workplace ethics, appropriate behavior in different contexts, cultural sensitivity, and creating a positive work environment intertwine to form a solid foundation for successful leadership and healthy relationships.

Ethics in the work environment is like a beacon, illuminating the right path. It is the set of moral values that guides us to make fair and honest decisions, showing that integrity is essential for respectable leadership.

Behaving appropriately in different contexts is like wearing the right clothes for the occasion. It is understanding the nuances of each environment, knowing how to behave, speak and act, which is essential to build solid relationships and make a positive impression.

Cultural sensitivity and inclusion are how to bridge differences. It is the ability to understand, respect and value diversity of perspectives, backgrounds and beliefs, creating an environment where everyone feels welcome and respected.

Showing empathy and care for others is like watering a garden so that the flowers will bloom. It's listening carefully, understanding colleagues' needs and feelings, and offering support when needed, which builds strong relationships and a cohesive team.

Creating a positive work environment is like turning on the lights in a dark room. It is to promote a climate of respect, recognition and encouragement, where collaboration and well-being are priorities, generating motivation and a sense of belonging.

Professional etiquette and empathy, understanding the importance of ethics, appropriate behavior, cultural sensitivity and creating a positive work environment. We will learn to apply these principles in a practical way, enhancing our ability to lead with integrity, adapt our behavior, value diversity, demonstrate genuine empathy, and cultivate an environment where everyone can grow and thrive. By mastering this perspective, we will be prepared to lead with impact, build healthy relationships and lead our team towards a positive and productive work environment where everyone can reach their best potential.

1. Ethics in the work environment

Ethics in the workplace are like the solid foundation of a building. It is the set of moral principles that guide our actions, decisions and interactions, creating an environment of trust, integrity and respect. In this chapter, we will explore the importance of ethics in the workplace, understanding how it is fundamental to respectable leadership and how we can apply these principles in our daily work.

Ethics is the pillar that sustains mutual trust between leaders and the team. It guides us to make fair and honest decisions, considering the impact of our actions on others and the work environment as a whole.

Integrity is the hallmark of an ethical leader. This means acting in accordance with our values, being transparent, honest and keeping our commitments, which inspires trust and respect.

Respect for others is a cornerstone of ethics. Treating everyone with consideration, valuing the diversity of opinions and showing empathy are attitudes that promote a healthy work environment.

Ethics also guide us in the pursuit of excellence. It encourages us to seek constant improvement, to make decisions that benefit the organization and to foster an environment where everyone can grow and prosper.

Ethics in the work environment, understanding the importance of integrity, respect, the pursuit of excellence and the positive impact that ethical leadership can have on the team and the organization. We will learn to apply these principles in our daily actions, strengthening our ability to lead with integrity, build trusting relationships and lead our team towards a work environment where everyone can feel valued and respected. By mastering this perspective, we will be prepared to lead with impact, creating a culture of ethics and respect that drives success and lasting growth.

2. Appropriate behavior in different contexts

In the world of leadership, knowing how to behave properly in different contexts is like having a versatile outfit that fits perfectly for every occasion. It is the ability to adapt our conduct, communication and posture to the circumstances, which allows us to build solid relationships and make a positive impression. In this chapter, we'll explore the importance of appropriate behavior in different contexts, understanding how this adaptability helps us to lead effectively, create meaningful connections, and achieve our goals.

Appropriate behavior is like speaking the right language in a multicultural environment. It's understanding the norms, values and expectations of each context, whether it's a formal meeting, a casual conversation or an important presentation.

Communication is a key to proper behavior. Knowing how to speak, listen and express our ideas in a clear and respectful way is essential to convey a professional image and gain the trust of others.

Posture is also essential. This involves the way we present ourselves, our tone of voice, our facial and body expressions, which can make all the difference in how we are perceived.

Adaptability is a strength of outstanding leaders. A leader who can adjust to different contexts, understand the nuances of each situation and act appropriately, demonstrates respect, consideration and leadership skills.

Leading by example is inspiring. A leader who shows how to behave properly, who values adaptability, effective communication and professional demeanor, creates a culture where everyone learns and benefits from this skill.

Appropriate behavior in different contexts, understanding the importance of adaptability, effective communication, posture and leadership by example. We will learn to apply these principles in different situations, improving our ability to lead successfully, build strong relationships and make a positive impression in any environment. By mastering this perspective, we will be prepared to lead with impact, adapt our behavior as needed and effectively lead our team in a variety of scenarios, achieving remarkable results.

3. Cultural sensitivity and inclusion

On the leadership journey, developing cultural sensitivity and promoting inclusion is like opening the door to a world of wealth and opportunity. It is the ability to understand and value different cultures, perspectives and experiences, creating an environment where everyone feels respected, recognized and able to contribute fully. In this chapter, we'll explore the importance of cultural sensitivity and inclusion, understanding how these elements are essential to effective leadership and how we can cultivate an environment where diversity is celebrated.

Cultural sensitivity is like speaking a universal language of respect. It is the ability to recognize cultural differences, understand the nuances of each individual's communication, behavior and values, and act with consideration and respect.

Promoting inclusion is building bridges between differences. It is to ensure that all voices are heard, that everyone has equal opportunities and that the work environment is welcoming, regardless of origin, gender, sexual orientation, religion or any other characteristic.

Celebrating diversity is a pillar of cultural sensitivity and inclusion. It is recognizing that each individual brings a unique set of experiences and talents, enriching the team and contributing to a more creative and innovative approach.

Inclusive leadership is inspiring. A leader who promotes cultural sensitivity and inclusion, who values diversity and creates an environment for collaboration, sets a powerful example for the team, fostering a sense of belonging and a climate of mutual respect.

Cultural sensitivity and inclusion in leadership, understanding the importance of recognizing and valuing differences, promoting equal opportunities and creating an environment where diversity is celebrated. We will learn to apply this approach to our leadership, improving our ability to lead with respect, build inclusive relationships and lead the team towards a culture of harmony, where everyone can feel valued and empowered to contribute their best. By mastering this perspective, we will be prepared to lead with impact, fostering a culture of respect, equality and inclusion that strengthens the team and drives lasting success.

4. Demonstrations of empathy and care for others

On the path of leadership, showing empathy and care for others is like lighting the way with kindness and understanding. It is the ability to put yourself in the shoes of others, recognize their needs, feelings and aspirations, creating an environment where everyone feels valued and supported. In this chapter, we'll explore the importance of showing empathy and caring for others, understanding how these gestures positively impact leadership and how we can cultivate an environment where human relationships are at the center of our attention.

Empathy is like an invisible hug, a connecting gesture that shows we care. It's the ability to understand others' perspectives, listen with genuine interest, and offer emotional support when needed.

Caring for others is a sign of responsible leadership. It is the attention dedicated to the needs and well-being of the team, which creates an environment where everyone feels cared for and valued, increasing motivation and a sense of belonging.

Empathetic communication is key. This means expressing genuine interest, demonstrating that we are available to listen, and creating an environment where colleagues feel comfortable sharing their thoughts, concerns, and ideas.

Attention to detail is a manifestation of care. Noticing effort, recognizing individual contributions and celebrating achievements are ways of showing that we value the dedication of each team member.

Leading by example is inspiring. A leader who shows empathy and care for others, who promotes an emotionally supportive environment, who values the well-being of the team, sets a standard of conduct that positively influences everyone around him.

Demonstrations of empathy and care for others in leadership, understanding the importance of listening, caring and emotionally supporting the team. We will learn to apply these principles in our leadership role, enhancing our ability to lead from the heart, build meaningful relationships and lead the team towards an environment where everyone feels valued and cared for. By mastering this perspective, we will be prepared to lead with impact, promoting an environment of trust, empathy and mutual support, which strengthens the team and brings remarkable results.

5. How to create a positive work environment

In the leadership scenario, creating a positive work environment is like planting seeds of prosperity and reaping the fruits of well-being and productivity. It's the art of building a place where people feel motivated, valued and engaged, resulting in a significant impact on the team's bottom line. In this chapter, we'll explore how to create a positive work environment, understanding the importance of an organizational climate, mutual support and a culture of respect, and how we can be agents of change to cultivate a space where everyone can thrive.

The organizational climate is the climate we breathe on a daily basis. It is the atmosphere that permeates the work environment, influencing the mood, motivation and satisfaction of the team. A positive organizational climate fosters a collaborative mindset, inspires innovation and strengthens commitment.

Mutual support is a solid foundation. A team that supports each other, shares knowledge, respects differences and helps each other grow, creates an environment where everyone feels part of something bigger and where overcoming challenges becomes a collective journey.

A culture of respect is like the glue that holds relationships together. It's valuing everyone's opinions and contributions, valuing diversity, creating an environment where everyone feels safe to express their ideas.

Recognition is a powerful motivator. Recognizing effort, celebrating achievements and valuing team work is a way to fuel motivation and create a sense of accomplishment and belonging.

Participative leadership is the cornerstone of a positive work environment. A leader who listens, supports, recognizes and inspires, creates a climate where everyone is aligned with the goals, feels valued and is willing to give their best.

Create a positive work environment, understanding the importance of an organizational climate, mutual support, a culture of respect and recognition. We will learn to apply these principles in our leadership, improving our ability to promote an environment of well-being and productivity, where everyone can grow and prosper. By mastering this perspective, we will be prepared to lead with impact, building an environment where the team feels motivated, valued and engaged, which leads to remarkable results and a healthy and inspiring organizational climate.

Chapter 10: Managing Your Soft Skills Development

On the leadership path, managing the development of your Soft Skills is like cultivating a garden of skills that flourish and enrich your journey. It is the art of evaluating, setting goals, seeking learning opportunities, practicing daily and monitoring progress, creating a virtuous cycle of personal and professional growth. In this chapter, we'll explore how to manage your own Soft Skills development, understanding the importance of assessment, planning, continuous learning and consistent practice to hone your skills and celebrate each step of your evolution.

Assessing your current Soft Skills is like doing a diagnostic to identify your strengths and areas for improvement. It's recognizing your communication skills, empathy, problem solving, leadership and other skills that make a difference in leadership.

Defining goals and action plans for development is to outline a roadmap for your growth. It's about setting clear goals, identifying the areas you want to improve and creating an action plan to achieve those goals, either through training, practices or challenging experiences.

Pursuing training and learning opportunities is like adding nutrients to the soil. It's looking for courses, workshops, books, mentoring and other sources of knowledge that provide the development of your Soft Skills, enriching your skills base.

Practicing the skills on a daily basis is like watering the seeds for their growth. It's applying the lessons learned in real situations, practicing effective communication, leadership, conflict resolution and other skills in your work environment and personal life.

Monitoring progress and celebrating growth is like reaping the rewards of your efforts. It's tracking progress towards established goals, making adjustments as needed, and celebrating each achievement, recognizing the value of your continued development.

Explore how to manage your Soft Skills development, understanding the importance of assessment, planning, continuous learning, practice and celebration of growth. We will learn to apply this cycle of development to our leadership trajectory, honing our skills, expanding our capacity for influence, and celebrating each step of our evolution as leaders. By mastering this perspective, we will be prepared to lead with impact, cultivate constant growth and achieve remarkable results, both for our own journey and for the team we lead towards success.

1. Assessing Your Current Soft Skills

Assessing your current Soft Skills is like taking an honest assessment of your skill sets that significantly influence your leadership journey. It is a moment of self-knowledge, where you analyze your communication skills, empathy, problem solving, teamwork and other capabilities that shape your ability to lead effectively.

Start by reflecting on recent situations where your Soft Skills were tested. Ask yourself: How well did you communicate complex ideas? How did you handle a conflict? How did you empathize with a colleague facing challenges? Examine your actions, reactions and the results obtained.

Soliciting feedback is also crucial. Ask colleagues, supervisors and team members to share their perceptions of your

Soft Skills. This outside perspective can reveal strengths you may not have noticed, as well as areas that can be improved.

Use assessment tools such as quizzes or tests that assess your leadership competencies and Soft Skills. This gives you an objective view of where you excel and where you can focus your development efforts.

Be honest with yourself. Acknowledge your areas of improvement without judgment, as the assessment process is an opportunity for growth, not a judgment on your worth as a leader.

By assessing your current Soft Skills, you are taking the first step towards continued development, honing your capabilities and preparing yourself to lead with impact. An honest understanding of your starting point will allow you to chart a solid plan to build more robust skills, achieving remarkable results along your leadership journey.

2. Defining goals and action plans for development

Setting Goals and Action Plans for Development: Charting the Path to Growth
Now that you've assessed your current Soft Skills, it's time to chart a clear path for development. Setting goals and creating action plans is like establishing a roadmap for improving your skills, ensuring that every step you take is targeted and strategic.

Start by setting specific, measurable goals. Your goals must be clear, achievable and with tangible success criteria. For example, if you want to improve your communication skills, your goal might be "Improve the clarity and impact of presentations as measured by positive feedback from colleagues after meetings".

Break your goals into smaller steps. Create a detailed action plan that outlines activities and deadlines to reach each milestone.

For example, your plan might include communication courses, regular presentation practice, and asking for feedback each month.

Be realistic about your time and resources. Take into account your current responsibilities and commitments so that your plan is achievable. Adaptability is key, but having a solid plan from the start will help you stay focused.

Seek learning and training opportunities. Search for courses, workshops, conferences, and online resources that align with your development goals. Be willing to learn from books, articles, and everyday experiences.

Consider finding a mentor or coach who can guide you. They can offer valuable insights, share experiences, and help you navigate challenges that arise during development.

With each step completed, celebrate your achievements. Acknowledge the progress you've made and use that motivation to keep moving towards your bigger goals.

By setting goals and action plans for developing your Soft Skills, you are building a solid plan for continued growth. This allows you to focus your efforts, track your progress, and direct your energies toward honing the skills that will make you a more effective leader. With a well thought out plan, you are well on your way to achieving remarkable results on your leadership journey.

3. Seeking training and learning opportunities

The pursuit of training and learning opportunities is like opening windows to new knowledge, skills and perspectives. It is an essential step in the development of your Soft Skills, providing a conducive environment to grow and evolve as a leader. In the process, you will expand your horizons, discovering valuable resources to enhance your skills.

Start by researching courses related to your development goals. Look for programs that focus on the specific skills you want to improve, such as communication, leadership, conflict resolution, and more. Online platforms, educational institutions, face-to-face workshops and professional development events are great sources of training.

Also consider the possibility of mentoring or coaching. Having an experienced mentor or coach who can guide you on your development journey can be extremely valuable. They can provide personalized guidance, share actionable insights, and help you tackle specific challenges.

Take advantage of resources available for free. There are many online materials such as articles, videos, podcasts and basic courses that can provide you with valuable information. Libraries, webinars, discussion groups and online forums are also rich sources of knowledge.

Participate in events and conferences related to your area of expertise. These events not only provide learning opportunities, but also allow you to interact with other professionals, expanding your network of contacts.

Be willing to learn from everyday experiences. Every interaction, challenge, or project in your work environment can be a learning opportunity. Be open to feedback, look at what works and what can be improved, and be willing to adapt and grow.

By pursuing training and learning opportunities, you are investing in your personal and professional growth. These opportunities can help you gain new perspectives, techniques and insights, enabling you to become a more skilled and effective leader. Keep an open mind, explore different sources of knowledge and be willing to dedicate yourself to the learning process. With that attitude, you're well on your way to achieving remarkable results on your leadership journey.

4. Practicing the skills in everyday life

Constant practice is the way to master your Soft Skills. It's like an athlete training every day to hone his skills. Through consistent practice, you internalize these competencies, making them a natural part of your approach as a leader. In this chapter, we'll explore the importance of practicing your skills on a daily basis and how this contributes to your continued development.

Integrate the skills into your everyday life. In every interaction, meeting, or task, consider how you can apply your Soft Skills. If you're working on a team, think about how you can promote clear communication and effective collaboration. If you're dealing with a challenge, think about how you can use your problem-solving and decision-making skills.

Ask for feedback regularly. Ask colleagues and team members to provide you with feedback on how you are applying your skills. Not only does this help you identify areas for improvement, it also demonstrates that you are committed to developing yourself.

Take initiatives to challenge yourself. Look for situations where you can apply your Soft Skills in a more challenging way. This may involve leading projects, dealing with conflict situations, or taking on responsibilities that stretch your competencies.

Be reflective. At the end of each day or week, reflect on how you applied your skills. What worked well? What could be improved? This ongoing self-assessment practice will help you adjust your focus and identify areas that need more attention.

Keep patience and persistence. Mastering Soft Skills doesn't happen overnight. It takes time and effort. Constant practice, even when facing challenges, is what will lead you to the level of proficiency you want to reach.

By practicing your skills day in and day out, you are building a solid foundation to become an exceptional leader. Each interaction, each challenge faced is an opportunity for growth. Constant practice not only hones your Soft Skills, it also increases your confidence and ability to lead with impact. Be committed to the practice and be willing to learn from each experience. With that commitment, you are well on your way to achieving remarkable results on your leadership journey.

5. Monitoring progress and celebrating growth

Tracking progress and celebrating growth is like charting your development and marking each achievement along the way. It's a vital practice to stay focused, measure progress and recognize the value of every effort you invest in evolving your Soft Skills. In this chapter, we'll explore the importance of tracking progress and how to celebrate each step of your growth as a leader.

Set clear milestones and metrics. Identify indicators that can measure the progress of your Soft Skills. This could include how often you apply a particular skill, the perceived improvement in the feedback you receive, or the ability to tackle challenges more effectively.

Keep a record of your development. Have a diary where you write down your experiences, learnings, challenges overcome and achievements. Not only does this help you track progress, but it also gives you valuable perspective when looking back.

Conduct regular assessments. Take moments to assess how well you are progressing towards your developmental goals. This can be done every quarter or every six months. Be honest with yourself and adjust your action plan as needed.

Celebrate every achievement, no matter how small. Every step towards improvement is an achievement that deserves recognition. Celebrate when you overcome a challenge, receive positive feedback, or see your skills successfully applied.

Share your achievements with others. By sharing your progress with colleagues, friends or mentors, you not only celebrate your achievements, but also inspire and motivate others.

Be patient with the process. The development of Soft Skills is continuous and non-linear. Some areas may evolve more quickly than others, and this is completely normal. The key is to keep moving forward.

By monitoring progress and celebrating growth, you recognize the value of your effort and motivate yourself to continue to improve your Soft Skills. Every step, no matter how small, is a step towards your ultimate goal of becoming an exceptional leader. Stay committed to development, value each achievement and be willing to learn from each experience. With this approach, you are well on your way to achieving remarkable results on your leadership journey.

We have reached the end of the book, to acquire new skills and different perspectives, new knowledge and new concepts, access the portfolio of Geo Report on Amazon and always stay up to date. Thanks for reading our books ;)